YOUR POCKET COACH
25 Powerful Reminders

Karen Gibbs

Your Pocket Coach © 2021 by Karen Gibbs
All rights reserved

Published by Author Academy Elite
PO Box 43, Powell, OH 43065

All rights reserved. This book contains material protected under international and federal copyright laws and treaties. Any unauthorized reprint or use of this material is prohibited. No part of this book may be reproduced or transmitted in any form or by any means, electronic or mechanical, including photocopying, recording, or by any information storage and retrieval system, without express written permission from the author.

Identifiers:
LCCN: 2021919913
Paperback: 978-1-64746-919-1
Hardback: 978-1-64746-920-7
eBook: 978-1-64746-921-4

Available in paperback, hardback and e-book.

All scripture quotations, unless otherwise indicated, are taken from the Holy Bible, New International Version®, NIV®. Copyright © 1973, 1978, 1984 by Biblica, Inc.™ Used by permission of Zondervan. All rights reserved world-wide.

This journal comes with further support.
Scan this QR code to connect with my
support groups or inspirational pages.

Find my book:
*Stop the Downward Spiral: Everything the
person in your life who struggles with
depression wishes you knew.*

www.linktr.ee/KarenGibbs
www.KarenGibbs.com.au

Hi there,

Today more than ever, we need to get connected and feel supported. Sometimes this is not physically possible, so it's good to have a coach in our pocket - right? By design, this little book is here to support you when no one else can. We know that connection is so important, so we need to adapt and thrive in this new way of life by being intentional with our thought processes.

I encourage you to focus on the words within this little book - really reflect on them and write out your thoughts and feelings to gain the full benefit.

For the eBook version, have a notepad handy before you begin. Then, you can refer to the motivational content repeatedly; the more you reflect, the more you will grow and heal. Your unique journey starts here - I encourage you to empower yourself.

From my heart to yours, Karen xx

25 Coaching Topics:

1. Anger
2. Anxiety
3. Feeling Down about Yourself
4. Bad Memories
5. Grief
6. Hope
7. Mental Strength
8. Creativity
9. Self-Care
10. Habits
11. Addiction
12. Suicidal Thoughts
13. Happiness
14. The Power of Today
15. Boundaries
16. Self-Forgiveness
17. Isolation
18. Your Comfort Zone
19. Self-Limiting Beliefs
20. Laughter
21. Celebrate Yourself
22. Unconditional Self-Love
23. Inspiration

24. Goals
25. Impossible to Possible

This little book can be used on its own or in conjunction with my book, *Stop the Downward Spiral,* which promotes strong mental health through connection and adventure.

Choose a topic or go through the book in any order which you feel comfortable. By writing it out you will find yourself changing, and clarity revealed. Journaling with gratitude in mind is very uplifting and writing is a great form of self-expression. Sometimes we are so caught up in life's issues that we can't see the wood for the trees, as the old saying goes. Let's change that today.

Anger

To free yourself from your internalised pain, think about the cause. The common causes of anger are rooted in fear, frustration, or insecurity. Are you feeling any of these emotions? Go deeper with your thoughts. Acting out of anger causes a deeper level of pain to boil over, leaving you feeling exposed and helpless.

> A man without self-control is like a city broken into and left without walls.
> —Proverbs 25:28

Breathe deeply and work through the hidden feelings within yourself to build a strong wall against further pain.

Jot those hidden feelings down.

"Trust your instincts."
– *Stop the Downward Spiral, Karen Gibbs*

2

Anxiety

The anxiety caused from your racing thoughts, palpitations, and sleeplessness cause you to feel stress—oftentimes even when you're excited. To break the habit, take some time each day to calm your thoughts. Take some deep breaths, let your shoulders drop, and unclench your jaw to begin healing.

> Anxiety in the heart of a man causes depression, but a good word makes it glad.
> —Proverbs 12:25

Is there something you feel indecisive about? Clearing that uncertainty up can alleviate your anxiety almost immediately.

Can you think of ten things you are grateful for today?

"Relax and unwind at intervals throughout the day to stop anxiety building."

3

Feeling Down about Yourself

Sadly, low self-esteem can become an issue when we feel down, leaving us open to bullies. Of course, we know the bullies are the ones with the problem, but it's hard to acknowledge that when our self-worth has taken a battering. This often leads us to become our own bullies over time when we start believing their insults and judgements.

> My grace is sufficient for you, for my power is made perfect in weakness. God is with you in times of need—consistently.
> —2 Corinthians 12:19

Repeat with confidence: I will not let my insecurities win. I am good enough. Yes!

Give yourself some grace and write a list of good things about yourself.

"You are unique. Don't let insecurities win!"

4

Bad Memories

We all have memories that affect us negatively, and unfortunately, our brain is wired to hang onto those with a stronger grip than the positive ones. This is likely because our brain must spend more energy understanding why such bad things need to happen in our life.

> I think it is right to refresh your memory as long as I live in the tent of this body.
> —2 Peter 1:13

Try to counteract that negativity with a positive takeaway from the experience. This will help promote healing.

Write down ten positive lessons you learned from an experience that triggers a negative memory.

"Replace negatives with positives.
Keep writing!"

5

Grief

We all experience grief and loss at some point in our lives, but we must take great care not to become part of what gets lost in that pain. It's easy to succumb to and even harder to heal from that pain. It often becomes so unbearable that the emotional pain turns into physical pain, attacking our bodies, hearts, and minds simultaneously.

> No pain is a waste.
> —Matty Gibbs

We can seek comfort from grief and loss by remembering the people and things we lose aren't lost forever. They leave a positive, indelible mark on our hearts, like a tattoo that covers the skin, protecting us from our loneliness and despair.

Dig deep into something that's caused you pain in the past.
How did this make you stronger?

"Dare to work towards fulfilling your dreams."

6

Hope

Our lives are full of ups and downs, and nobody has a life free of pain. To survive the rough patches when they come, we must hold onto hope that tomorrow will feel a bit lighter. And maybe the next day, we will feel even lighter and more hopeful than that. Without hope, our heart is in danger of withering away and succumbing to depression.

> You will be secure,
> because there is hope;
> you will look about you
> and take your rest in
> safety.
> —Job 11:18

Close your eyes and hope for a better tomorrow; you have everything to gain. The best is yet to come!

Write about a loved one who makes you feel hopeful.
What have they taught you that makes you look forward to your future?

"You matter, you are loved!"

7

Mental Strength

Because you are strong, you are more likely to experience depression or anxiety because you lack the desire to give up on achieving your dreams or pursuing happiness. Sometimes, it is rather exhausting, but we need to take care while pushing forward with our strong minds.

> Blessed is the one who perseveres under trial because, having stood the test, that person will receive the crown of life.
> —James 1:12

Find solace in the fact that your strength lies in your heart for a purpose: it is not there to allow you to give up before you reach the finish line.

Write down five thoughts that make you feel strong.
Return to this journal and reread whenever your strength feels like it's fading.

"Enjoy the moments, for these moments become your life" – *Matty Gibbs*

8

Creativity

Like many of you, my youngest son, Matty, struggled with depression, anxiety, and low self-esteem. But, on the other hand, he was the most creative person I ever knew. He had such a gift for turning his pain into purpose. After his passing, I learned how powerfully therapeutic creative writing could be when I wrote my book, Stop the Downward Spiral. Like Matty, many of you reading this also have a gift for words— or painting, photography, crafting, design, acting, etc.

> If I couldn't write, life would have no purpose.
> —Matty Gibbs

Use your creativity every day to free the part of you that needs to connect with others.

Write down five ideas for creative projects you could work on to distract yourself from what's holding you back or causing anxiety in your life.

"Perhaps try something new; List something here that you'd like to try."

9

Self-Care

If you're someone who spends a lot of time caring for others, you probably don't think much about taking extra time to care for yourself. No matter how hard it is to find the time or strength, you must take time to do this! Schedule it on your calendar if you need to—just make sure you're actively loving yourself each day.

> To love oneself is the beginning of a lifelong romance.
> —Oscar Wilde, *An Ideal Husband*

Self-care is everything you do to take care of your physical and mental health. It can be anything small or large, and it doesn't have to cost any money.

For the next week, write down at least one thing you did every day to care for yourself.

"Remember, self-care is essential
- not selfish."

10

Habits

Some habits you have are beneficial to you, but it's likely you hold onto others that harm you. Over time, these negative habits can create more stress, depression, and anxiety. Three simple words can derail those bad habits—UP UNTIL NOW . . .

> "I have the right to do anything," you say—but not everything is beneficial. "I have the right to do anything"—but I will not be mastered by anything.
> —1 Corinthians 6:12

What bad habits are holding you back?

Focus on a negative habit you'd like to change and write out ten *"UP UNTIL NOW"* statements to gain courage to change them.

"Your future will change for the better. List what you feel could improve your future."

11

Addiction

For people who suffer from anxiety and depression, addiction is an unfortunate possible side effect. We often think we're doing better when we self-medicate, but over the years, the stress that adds to our bodies and minds builds and creates more problems in our lives.

> It teaches us to say "No" to ungodliness and worldly passions, and to live self-controlled, upright and godly lives in this present age.
> —Titus 2:12

Make a commitment to yourself not to self-medicate, no matter what it takes to persevere.

Write down five alternatives to alcohol and drugs you can turn to during times of great stress, anxiety, or depression.

"Reach out and stay connected in a healthy manner. How could you do this?"

#　12

Suicidal Thoughts

The most devastating side effect of depression is the onset of suicidal thoughts. These thoughts don't care how much we have to live for; they simply want to destroy all hope and possibility.

> "For I know the plans I have for you," declares the Lord, "plans to prosper you and not to harm you, plans to give you hope and a future."
> —Jeremiah 29:11

Connect daily and intentionally with things that make you feel hopeful of counteracting the thoughts that might lead you to contemplate suicide. You are loved.

Write down the names and contact information of five people you can reach out to when a negative thought hits.

"Remember there are many support groups who want to help 24/7. Write the contact details for those in your area. Don't hesitate to call if needed."

13

Happiness

The point of holding onto hope and moving forward is not to attain that final reward of happiness. Nobody can sustain a feeling of happiness all the time, but we will have many moments full of joy and peace. The point is to find a way to enjoy those moments despite the moments that try to rip us apart.

> As servants of God we commend ourselves in every way . . . sorrowful, yet always rejoicing; poor, yet making many rich; having nothing, and yet possessing everything.
> —2 Corinthians 6:4,10

Rejoice in those small moments of joy to keep you going.

Express gratitude by writing about three moments of joy you've experienced today. Reflect on how that shifts your attitude about your ability to attain happiness.

"Attitude is everything, but it needs to be built up. You've got this!"

14

The Power of Today

Today is much more than a day in the span of your personal history. It's a chance to reflect on not how far you have to go—but on how far you've come from yesterday. You can experience great joy in all your accomplishments if you can look at what you have and what you're doing in comparison to what you *had* and what you *did* yesterday, one year ago, or ten years ago. It's important to reflect on the differences because it can help you keep moving forward to a much better tomorrow.

> If you fell down yesterday, stand up today.
> —H.G. Wells

The past is not the present, so let your future live.

Write down at least three ways that something in your life is more positive today than it was one year ago.

"Today is what's important."

15

Boundaries

One of the most important ways you can care for yourself is through setting healthy boundaries. Our lives get so busy with obligations and responsibilities that we don't stop to think that maybe we aren't superhuman. This is especially true for parents who don't like to disappoint others. Of course, in a perfect world, we'd want to do everything people ask of us, but it's not always realistic. It's ok—and necessary—to set boundaries to give ourselves room to breathe and enjoy our lives.

> No is a complete sentence.
> —Anne Lamont

Saying *no* is not a weakness; it's a self-care requirement.

What boundaries can you set today that will help you reduce the stress in your life?

"Taking time to rest your body and mind is important too."

16

Self-Forgiveness

We all make mistakes; some of us even make them every day. But it's essential that we not define ourselves by those mistakes. Instead, think of them as a few steps off the beaten track that showed you what you didn't want. So first, forgive yourself for your misstep, then correct your path and try again.

> I think that if God forgives us, we must forgive ourselves. Otherwise, it is almost like setting up ourselves as a higher tribunal than him.
> —CS Lewis

If you can forgive others, you can forgive yourself. Start by letting your loved ones guide you through their own forgiveness.

What thought, mistake, event, or behaviour do you need to forgive yourself for? Write about how it would change your life if you could find a path to forgiveness.

"Treat yourself with care and kindness, just as you want others to treat you."

17

Isolation

When we feel depressed, we are often more inclined to isolate ourselves from the rest of the world. It makes us feel better at first, but over time, the isolation holds us captive, gradually making our anxiety and depression worse. It's fine to enjoy having some alone time, but when we isolate for days at a time, we run the risk of making it a permanent habit. Then, the next thing we know, we start having panic attacks every time there's a need to leave the house.

> It begins with isolation—demons always inhabit desolate places.
> —John Geddes, *A Familiar Rain*

If you find yourself isolating, look for activities that involve other people.

What do you think the difference is between spending some time alone and isolation? What one thing will you do today that allows you to engage with the outside world?

"Maintain balance in everything you do."

18

Your Comfort Zone

Comfort zones feel nice, don't they? Well, they should—they're comfortable! They are nice tools to use whenever we feel as though we're in danger, but they can become crutches that keep us from growing. True transformation takes place when we step outside our comfort zones, no matter how intolerable it feels.

> Have I not commanded you? Be strong and courageous. Do not be afraid; do not be discouraged, for the Lord your God will be with you wherever you go.
> —Joshua 1:9

It's okay to stand in your comfort zone, but you shouldn't make a habit of staying there.

What will you do this week to step outside your comfort zone?
After you do, come back to your journal to write about how it made you feel.

"Your comfort zone grows bigger with each accomplishment."

19

Self-Limiting Beliefs

We all suffer from a shallow belief in ourselves from time to time, and if we spend too much time focusing on those limiting thoughts, they turn into truths in our minds. These thoughts can derail us from our goals and dreams, so we need to be careful not to let them live in our minds for long. If we do, those limiting beliefs become confirmed, and it's much harder to fix the damage they've done.

> Whatever the mind can conceive and believe, the mind can achieve.
> —Napoleon Hill, *Think and Grow Rich*

Counteract your self-limiting beliefs with self-affirming beliefs by remembering a time you achieved a hard goal.

Write down a self-limiting belief of yours, then cross it out.
Underneath that old belief, write something positive that affirms your belief in yourself.

"It's normal to feel down at times, but practise saying great things about yourself and see how much better you feel. Your body believes everything you think."

20

Laughter

I like to watch short, silly videos when I'm feeling stressed or depressed because it gives me a nice reprieve from the mental anguish. Medical experts even believe laughter can boost our immune system, relieve physical pain, and even improve our circulation.

> Our mouths were filled with laughter, our tongues with songs of joy. Then it was said among the nations, "The Lord has done great things for them."
>
> —Psalm 126:2

Have you laughed yet today? Take a few minutes to give yourself the gift of joy.

What is your favourite sitcom or funny movie? How does it make you feel when you watch it?

"Capture that happy feeling, and *LOL* for real today!"

21

Celebrate Yourself

In all of the world, there is nobody who has been born quite like you or me. We may feel down on ourselves once in a while, but we are worth celebrating. Celebrate your survival. Celebrate your joy. Celebrate your successes. Celebrate your significance. It's all worth praising because there is nobody alive on this planet quite like you.

> The real difficulty is to overcome how you think about yourself.
> —Maya Angelou

This is the only *you* you will ever get. Celebrate that fact every day because you are special, important, and unique.

Write down ten things you want to celebrate about yourself. Add one thing to this list every day for a year.

"Celebrate the small wins as they arrive!"

22

Unconditional Self-Love

We talk about loving other people unconditionally, but how often do we offer that love to ourselves? Out of anyone in our lives, we deserve to give ourselves unconditional love. This is not selfish—this is powerful. When you love yourself without question, you'll be able to move mountains to achieve your goals and dreams, and you'll also be able to help others do this as well.

> Love yourself first and everything else falls into line.
> —Lucille Ball

Find little ways every day to fall madly in love with yourself time and time again. Soon, you'll wonder why you spent so much time disliking yourself.

How would your life change if you loved yourself unconditionally?

"What you focus your mind on is the key to what you unlock in life" – *Karen Gibbs*

23

Inspiration

There is one thing we can cling to for comfort: we are never alone in this world. So, whether you choose to walk with Jesus or look to your friends and family for support, you will find inspiration all around to lift you, motivate you to better yourself, and push you toward pursuing your dreams.

> I can do all this through him who gives me strength.
> —Philippians 4:13

Even the smallest things can inspire us to find, hope, joy, peace, and comfort. Look for these things every day. They are worth celebrating!

Who inspires you to be a better person?
How have they changed your life?

"You are not alone."

24

Goals

We all have goals and dreams we aspire to work toward, but life often gets in the way. The most successful people don't allow distractions to stop them from pursuing their goals—even if it takes a decade to get there. Five minutes a day working on your goals can make a difference if you can open your mind wide enough to acknowledge you deserve to pursue your dreams.

> When you want to succeed as bad as you want to breathe, then you'll be successful.
> —Eric Thomas, *The Secret to Success*

Don't waste any more time ignoring where you want to go in life. Your future starts today—let's get going!

Write down five goals you want to achieve this year. Next, write one little thing you can do today for each of your goals to get started on them.

"Hope is Eternal, never give up"
- *Matty Gibbs*

25

Impossible

So many things in our life feel insurmountable—impossible. But it gives me a great deal of hope to see that the word *possible* can be found in everything we feel is impossible. On the surface, this is a negative word, but we can change that today through some positive mantras:

It is impossible for me to lose hope.
It is impossible for me to hurt others.
It is impossible for me to lose my joy.

> Impossible is not a fact.
> It's an opinion.
> —Muhammad Ali

You can take back the word *impossible* by flipping it around to say: *It is impossible for me to fail.*

What would you do today if it was impossible to fail? Tomorrow? Next year?

"You've got this!"

Stop the Downward Spiral
is available on Amazon:
www.amazon.com/author/karengibbs

www.linktr.ee/KarenGibbs

This is really the beginning of a brighter future. Hope to hear from you in one of my groups soon. - *Karen xx*

www.ingramcontent.com/pod-product-compliance
Lightning Source LLC
LaVergne TN
LVHW011846060526
838200LV00054B/4187